"*Change Is a Ju...*

organization faces—change! While change can be diffi-cult, this book provides straightforward and practical ideas about how each of us fit within the jungle of change. From having Terry present this at a recent conference, I can attest to the benefits your team will have in understanding their change type to stay on mission."

Don Bishop
CEO, SR Management Companies
Tallahassee, Florida

"Terry Wright gives us an insightful, engaging, and en-tertaining discussion of inevitable change as he pre-sents an approach that allows us to easily identify how we individually adapt to change. By using various ani-mal characteristics to help us discern our reaction to change, he encourages us not to allow change to stress us but instead to approach inevitable change as an op-portunity for growth. I enjoyed reading this book and encourage you to read it as well."

Omar L. Hamada, MD, MBA, MATS, FAAFP, FACOG, FICS
Adjunct Professor, Union University,
McAfee School of Business
Clinical Associate Professor, Belmont University,
Thomas F. Frist, Jr. College of Medicine,
Department of Integrated Clinical Education

"Every day we face changes in our lives, whether big or small. And more so as society changes, we sometimes struggle with finding the good or accepting the new normal. Terry's book helps us to embrace the change, to filter the noise, and to look at things with clarity so we can learn, grow, and survive the jungle of life."

Charlie Matthews
Director of Ambulatory Operations,
Graduate Medical Education, HCA Healthcare
Nashville, Tennessee

Change Is a Jungle

It's Who You Are and Who's around You That Gets You Through

Change Is a Jungle

It's Who You Are and Who's around You That Gets You Through

Terry Wright

To my wife Renee and my kids, Madison, Carson, and Parker: you guys have stuck with me through a whole lot of change.

Table of Contents

Introduction

"Only I can change my life. No one can do it for me."

—Carol Burnett, comedian

LET'S BE HONEST. We all hate two things in life: change and the same ol' thing! It's hard to embrace change, and it's easy to become complacent with the status quo. To complicate the dilemma, our world is in a constant state of change. Just look at how much change has been thrust on us in the past 110 years.

Change: It's Been Going On for Years

Think about the changes in America since 1910.

	1910	Today
Average life expectancy	47 years	70 years
Percentage of homes with a bathtub	14	99
Cars on the road	8,000	253 million

1

Miles of paved roads	144	4 million
Maximum speed limit in most cities	10 mph	70 mph
Percentage of home births	95	1.3
Percentage of physicians with no college education	90[i]	0
Price of coffee	15¢/lb.	$7/lb.

Change is always in the air, and it gets personal. We see change in our health, our relationships, our workplace, and, really, every place we go. Change subscribes to that old cliché: it's not a matter of if; it's a matter of when. Since change is inevitable, how are we going to handle it?

When faced with the inevitable, we like to play one of humanity's most popular indoor sports: comparison. We look around at how others navigate change. They change jobs, houses, relationships, hobbies, and a whole lot of et cetera. And they either navigate it with grace or with even greater paralysis than we do. We judge how well we navigate change by comparing ourselves to others navigating similar situations.

Why do some people embrace change with relative ease while others struggle? That's the question I want to tackle in this book. I can promise you this: reading this book thoughtfully will help you process change more quickly and yield better outcomes than simply coasting through your next uninvited fork in the road. If you are a leader, reading this little book will give you a better understanding of the people you lead and how they process and adapt to change.

> **Why do some people embrace change with relative ease while others struggle?**

My strategy is simple: I am going to compare the world of change to a jungle and show you how different jungle dwellers are hardwired to handle the jungle. Along the way there will be short assessments to help you discover how you are hardwired to handle change. Take a minute and go through the questions. They will help you. I promise.

I categorize these personality types in terms of four jungle dwellers: jaguars, chameleons, sloths, and hippos. Yep, you're one of those four. Don't be offended if you discover you are a sloth or a hippo—it's not personal! All four personalities have great value and are needed on every team.

You will be amazed at how reading this little book will help you navigate your jungle of change. And I hope you have fun along the way!

"Some changes look negative on the surface but you will soon realize that space is being created in your life for something new to emerge."

—Eckhart Tolle

Part 1

Change

Change (n.): "to make the form, nature, content, future course, etc., of (something) different from what it is or from what it would be if left alone . . . to become different . . . altered."[ii]

WE RELATE TO EACH other through shared experiences: we love our kids; we value hard work; we dream about retirement; and we want to lose a little weight! But there are few experiences we *all* share. Uninvited change is one of the few universal unifiers.

As John F. Kennedy reminded us, "Change is the law of life. And those who look only to the past or present are certain to miss the future."[iii] Calling it the "law of life" frames change correctly: it will come knocking on your door soon enough.

Change may produce a myriad of feelings, some good and others not so good. The person in the cubicle next to you may thrive on it. You, however, may struggle with anxiety, depression, fear, or even sadness at its prospect.

> **Uninvited change is one of the few universal unifiers.**

Why does change cause such extreme reactions? Let's define it and figure out why.

What Is Change?

In the TV show *The Wonder Years*, the narrator routinely became the voice of wisdom about the path through life. In one episode, he shared, "Change is never easy. You fight to hold on. You fight to let go."[iv]

The holding on and letting go plays out like this: we select a career and climb the ladder; we fall in love, marry, and begin raising a family; we work out and eat well (at least enough to keep our doctor happy). Then something changes. We get fired from the job we've held for years. Our "forever relationships" wither. Our doctor orders some tests . . .

We're content living in our jungle, and then change shows up. You might say the vines of change impede our happy path. It happens to everyone.

We recognize that change is common, but we fool ourselves to believe that change doesn't touch some people—like those in positions of power or wealth. We want to join this "protected" class. We convince our-selves that if we could just break into *that* group, change would not touch us. But *that* group doesn't ex-ist. Change is the universal unifier: it is the law of life—even for the rich and famous.

Industrialist Henry Ford is a classic example. As inventor of the Ford Model T, he ushered in some of the most meaningful change in the twentieth century, but his preference was to cling to the status quo. Re-garding the color of vehicles, Ford said, "Any customer can have a car painted any color he wants, so long as it is black."[v]

Ford wasn't just resistant to change—he did all he could to stifle it. He believed in his heart of hearts that by the sheer force of his will he could shield his company, which he had worked so hard to build, from any change.

In 1912, after returning home from a trip abroad, Henry Ford went to the Highland Park garage to see what was happening within his successful com-pany. William Knudsen, Ford's production manager, had propelled the company's production efficiencies to new heights. Knudsen knew that the Model T, which was now four years old, was losing its appeal with the American consumer. Being a creative thinker and loyal employee, he made some sporty changes to Henry's black yet beloved Model T.

Upon Ford's arrival at the garage, Knudsen presented a shiny, newly designed red prototype for Mr. Ford's approval. Based on the accounts of the eyewitnesses, Mr. Ford walked around the car, looked carefully at each of the four bright red doors, gazed intently at the lower profile body, and opened one of the doors. Then, to the amazement of all, he ripped the door off its hinges. He proceeded to do the same to the other three doors.[vi]

It's fair to say the man who ushered in some of the most significant changes of the twentieth century resisted change himself.

But change didn't give Henry Ford a choice. Within two years, Ford had come around, and his production lines were cranking out the upgraded model known as the Model A.

Henry Ford was one of our nation's greatest industrialists and businessmen, a global leader by every measure. He resisted change with his whole heart, but in the end, he realized he needed to embrace it.

Change can be difficult, even for great leaders.

"He who rejects change is the architect of decay. The only human institution which rejects progress is the cemetery."

—Harold Wilson

The Jungle

Everyone lives in a jungle.

RESISTANCE TO CHANGE is always present. If you think about it, a jungle is a surprisingly good picture of how change looks as we hack through life. After all, a jungle is an "impenetrable thicket or tangled mass,"[vii] and we often see change as a problem or roadblock to our growth. Think of it like this: the jungle is anything and everything that causes us pain and frustration associated with change.

Similarities in All Jungles

I'm so thankful that every person is unique. Life would be dull if everyone were the same. However, when it comes to the jungle, most of us will face similar obstacles: ruts, rituals, relationships, and reality.

11

Ruts

A rut is a habit or pattern of behavior that has become unproductive. Despite their dullness and lack of productivity, ruts are hard to change because we've learned to love and trust them. I once heard John Maxwell say, "Ruts are like a great bed: easy to get into and hard to get out of." Vance Havner expanded on that thought, saying "a rut is simply a grave with both ends kicked out."

Think of it like this: the jungle is anything and everything that causes us pain and frustration associated with change.

A rut's repetitious acts can be on the personal level or embedded in our corporations. Many great companies begin to fail because they do things the way they've always done them. (Henry Ford almost ran the company into the rut of the black Model T.) Ruts are impossible to escape unless we are willing to change.

Why are ruts so appealing?

1. Comfortable Feelings

Remaining in a predictable rut is appealing because it offers reassurance in the form of peace, ease, comfort, confidence, et cetera. We can become addicted to these feelings. We know from biology that pleasant feelings are associated with the areas of our brains where hormones are released. A repeated positive stimulus can trigger the release of endorphins, serotonin, and dopamine, the feel-good anatomical chemicals. A rut's predictability and ease can train our brains to release these chemicals, causing us to appreciate rut living. These comfortable feelings mimic a sedative and keep us anchored to our destructive ways. As you've likely experienced, when you feel at peace, at ease, or comforted by the predictable, why would you seek to change?

2. Security and Control

Not only are ruts comfortable, but they also help us stay in control of our environment. Control and security go hand in hand. If you are the type who likes control, your desire for security is probably the reason why.

Almost everyone likes to be secure. (And the older we get, the more we fight for that feeling.) When someone feels secure, they feel safe. When times are uncertain due to rapid change, we tend to fight for safety and security.

A rut is repeated action. If you do anything over and over, you begin to feel like you know what you're doing. So ruts help build an identity of security within and around us. As change factors push us toward unknown territories, staying in a rut helps us maintain the sense—or at least the illusion—of control. If you stay in your rut while those around you are struggling through their jungles, you remain comfortable, safe, and in control while you watch them spiral unchecked.

3. Less Stress

By staying stuck in a rut, you think you're minimizing stress. Your thinking goes like this: *If I don't change, then I won't have to think new thoughts, learn new skills, or grow. Therefore, sameness equals no stress.*

Read that thought again. Logic will tell you that rationale is flawed, but your emotions take comfort in the routine, and that's all that matters.

Operating in ruts can eventually lead to your failure to see what is going on outside of your world. You know the old saying "ignorance is bliss"? Remaining in a rut fosters such ignorance.

Robert H. Schuller put it best when he said, "It takes guts to get out of ruts."[viii]

Rituals

Another obstacle common to everyone's jungle are rituals. Rituals are similar to ruts, but rituals are habits you follow with the additional twist of religious devotion. Rooted in a person's faith, they are habits on which you have become emotionally connected and dependent. You know something has become a ritual when a suggestion to change that behavior seems insulting and offensive. You have repeated these actions so often that they have become part of your psychological identity.

Rituals can develop in many areas—in church, of course, but also in relationships, family, clubs, the workplace, et cetera. They are connected to the emotional and often spiritual parts of life. The power of a ritual is real.

Rituals can also serve as anchors when your world is changing or falling apart. You default to them to find satisfaction and peace. Rituals have the power to keep you where you are, but they also have an almost supernatural ability to develop or transform you. Rituals become your identity and can even determine your sense of worth.

Given that authority, changing a ritual can mean changing the very way you see yourself and wish to be seen by others. Accordingly, if held too tightly, they can become snares that keep you from changing when it is essential to do so: rituals that keep you safe today can trap you tomorrow.

> *Rituals can also serve as anchors when your world is changing or falling apart.*

Relationships

Relationships are another element common to everyone's jungle. Let's keep this simple by defining relationship as "being connected." You know the power of relationships. People in your life have helped you get to where you are, and they sometimes know where you are going better than you do. It's natural for those people to become a vital part of your life. You have grown to love them, sometimes more than yourself. You cannot imagine life without their voice of wisdom to guide you.

When you are faced with the prospect of change, however, you may have to risk upsetting the people you care about in order to grow. Of all the vines and branches in the jungle, relationships can be the hardest to cut out of the way when change is needed.

This is often a sad part of the jungle. Some people want to keep you trapped in *their* rut for *their* benefit. Others may not understand why you are considering changing. If you are part of their ritual, for instance, your absence would spoil it. It will be hard for them to handle.

> **You may have to risk upsetting the people you care about in order to grow.**

Though difficult, you may have to love them through the jungle while simultaneously embracing the change you are going through. Change may require you to move away from the hometown you grew up in to accept a promotion, to continue to grow as a person, or simply to enjoy the adventure.

You will need the courage to say goodbye and the compassion to stay in touch.

Realities

No matter the jungle, reality is an ever-present obstacle.

Reality is easy to observe but hard to accept. It is the way things are, not the way you want things to be. You may look around and want things to be different, but reality denotes what actually exists.

Reality is easy to observe but hard to accept.

Like it or not, everyone must face reality at some point, but how each person handles reality varies. Reality can get on our last nerve. To win through change, we must recognize and admit what stands in the way. The jungle—and its harshest truths—is best faced with honesty, openness, and with an optimistic attitude. Following is a list of universal certainties that appear in all our jungles:

- *Age.* Age can be a blessing or a curse. The older you get, the slower you change. With all the rapid and regular change in technology, communication, and how you connect, the learning curve can be tough. However, as we age, we tend to understand and handle relationships better. So aging is both a blessing and a curse at times.

- *Motivation.* Everyone I know, even the most motivated, faces times when their motivation wanes. You want to be productive, but be honest

17

with yourself: sometimes, it is hard to get off the couch and get things done.

- *Diminishing Skills.* The older you get, the more you'll notice you are not what you used to be! Your skills are not as sharp. Your reaction time will ebb. Your ability to learn and assimilate material will fade.

- *Precipitous Change.* The world is speeding up. Technology is driving hurried changes in how we work, build relationships, communicate, go to school, shop, and so on. And guess what? There is no end to the increasing rapidity of our ever-changing world.

Ruts, rituals, relationships, and realities. Virtually every jungle has these elements, and they can become significant barriers to change. That's what makes your jungle an "impenetrable thicket or tangled mass."[ix]

But don't despair! Change may be the very thing that forces you to face the roadblocks and adapt. Sure, making your way through the thicket might be difficult, but hopefully you have been successfully navigating change most of your life.

To assist you in navigating the tangled mass of change, I suggest seven laws of the jungle.

Laws of the Jungle

Things to remember as you move through the jungle.

1. The jungle is alive and changing.

The circumstances you are going to face will flux and commingle constantly. Life is not static; it does not stand still. All the factors that create your personal jungle will be continually changing.

2. It's hard to move through the jungle.

Regardless of how often you have faced change or how good you may be at it, moving through the jungle is hard work. You will get tired. It is important to incorporate some breaks. In an interview, Rick Warren suggested everyone should "divert daily, withdraw weekly, and abandon annually."[x] He also said, "If you do not come apart, you will come apart."

3. Jungles are dangerous. Don't go it alone.

One thing I've learned in thirty years of leading and being a part of change is that there is always someone smarter than I am. Bring them along if you can. The jungle is filled with hidden dangers, and traveling alone is not the best way to do it. Take people who have different points of view than you; they may help you further down the road. King Solomon, in his book of wisdom, said, "But woe to him who is alone when he falls and has not another to lift him up!" (Eccles. 4:10). You will need friends in the jungle. Do not go it alone.

4. It's going to take resources to make it through the jungle.

Every great journey has to be fueled by the right resources. The number one reason well-designed start-up businesses fail is insufficient resources. Think deeply about what you may need as you start on your journey of change. Think also about what you can leave behind.

5. It's about persistence.

This law of the jungle is simple: don't quit.

6. It's not personal.

When moving through change, people may snipe at you. Never take it personally. It does not matter how they meant it. Decide ahead of time not to take it personally.

> *Think deeply about what you may need as you start on your journey of change. Think also about what you can leave behind.*

7. It's unique.

Let's be honest, it's hard not to compare ourselves to others. When we know of someone who has gone through something like we have, we compare. If it was easy for them, it should be easy for us, right? But our jungle is ours, not theirs. We are working through *our* ruts, rituals, relationships, and realities. Embrace the uniqueness and avoid the comparison game. Comparing will drain you of energy, vision, and desire.

> **Comparing will drain you of energy, vision, and desire.**

Now that you've been introduced to the jungle and have identified some of the qualities of your jungle, it's time to identify your change type.

Are you a jaguar, chameleon, sloth, or hippo? Let's find out!

Part 2

One Jungle; Different Animals

OVER THE PAST THIRTY years, I've observed two extremes when it comes to the jungle of change. One person faces significant change and moves through it pretty well. Another—facing the same situation—becomes paralyzed. Why did the same change factors impact them differently?

I've come to believe there are different personality types when it comes to adapting to change. Think about the various species that live in any jungle: jaguars, hippos, sloths, et cetera. Each possesses a hardwired personality. A jaguar acts like a jaguar because he is a jaguar. The same holds true for the others, and it holds true for you,

> *One person faces significant change and moves through it pretty well. Another—facing the same situation—becomes paralyzed.*

too. Your initial reactions to change are driven by your personality type.

Let's have a little fun as we explore personality types in terms of four jungle species: jaguars, chameleons, sloths, and hippos.

The Jaguar

JAGUARS ARE AS dangerous as they are beautiful. They are apex predators and a keystone species. In other words, they are at the top of their food chain. In its habitat, no animal gets the drop on this cat! As a keystone species, jaguars represent one of the smallest percentages of jungle species, but their predatorial nature makes their impact staggering. Think about it: there are fewer jaguars than almost any other species, but due to their tenacity, survivability, and hunting prowess, jaguars don't merely survive: they greatly impact the sustainability of other species.

To see the jaguar in its natural habitat would generally be unimpressive. Most of the time, jaguars are relaxed. They survey their surroundings. They try not to burn up calories. Yet, when the undergrowth rustles, when the need arises or an opportunity presents itself, jaguars demonstrate speed, agility, and power. They can pounce nineteen feet from the sitting position. They can reach sixty miles per hour in just seconds.

Rest assured, when the jaguar engages, there will be a body count.

On Your Team

You probably know at least one jaguar in your life. You might be one yourself. When a new software system is introduced at work, jaguars are the first to master it. When offices are flipped around, they have their stuff moved first. When the doctor tells them to change their diet, they change it on the fly. Jaguars thrive on change. When no change is necessary, they sit back—relaxed with no worries. Then change rustles in the brush, and the jaguars pounce!

Jaguars are excited about change. Movement and motion fill them with meaning and purpose. They may not even know what rustled in the brush—they simply know the hunt is on, and they want to lead the way. Their competitive juices flow, and they want to be the first ones called into immediate action. When jaguar personalities smell change, every cell in their bodies comes alive. They want to win no matter what or who is in the way.

> *Jaguars are excited about change. Movement and motion fill them with meaning and purpose.*

The great things about jaguars:

- Quick response to opportunity
- Eagerness to adapt
- Energy to initiate
- Strength to break through barriers
- Stamina to see a process through
- Agility on the run and ability to change directions
- Visibility inspires others

But these strong, agile agents of change come with some blind spots. The following are general tendencies that can be true for jaguars, to varying degrees.

The not-so-great things about jaguars:

- Disengaged when not challenged
- Can be hurtful to individuals and teams
- Can be blind to details
- Ambitious to the exclusion of others
- Deaf to feedback
- Oblivious to corporate memory

A self-assessment is on the next page. Answer the questions honestly to discover your jaguar tendencies.

Self-Assessment

1. When change is in the air how do you feel?

   4 Excited!

   3 Energized but cautious.

   2 Antsy and a bit overwhelmed.

   1 Anxious.

2. How did you approach your last change?

   4 With gusto!

   3 With some excitement.

   2 I did what I had to, but I did it reluctantly.

   1 I put off the changes till the last minute.

3. What is your opinion on positive change?

   4 I try to create positive change whenever I can!

   3 I am optimistic about what the change will mean.

   2 It's favorable, but I don't enjoy the process.

   1 It bothers me, but I make it through.

4. When offered opportunities (new relationships, a new job, a new house, etc.), which phrase summarizes your reaction?

   4 Love it!

   3 This could be great.

   2 It looks like a lot of work.

   1 Do I have to?

5. Do you get bored if things stay the same?

    4 Yes.

    3 Sometimes.

    2 Hardly ever.

    1 Never. I love consistency.

6. Have you ever initiated a major change in your life?

    4 Yes, many!

    3 Yes, but I try to balance it with being con-sistent.

    2 I prefer not to, but I do it when I have to.

    1 No. I avoid it at all costs.

Decoding Your Answers

Total your numbers. The max number is 24. The closer you are to 24, the more jaguar tendencies you possess. When change presents itself, if you are excited, energized, and feel adventurous, you have strong jaguar tendencies.

Life as a Jaguar

If you are displaying jaguar tendencies, you need to know something: many folks will shy away from you. It's not personal. It's survival. A leader who is not a jaguar may resent you. A spouse who is another personality type may resist your quick thinking.

Jaguars tend to be in front of the pack most of the time. They pursue change and want to transition quickly. But jaguars need to pace themselves when pursuing the change they desperately want. They must understand how much and the rate at which the organization can assimilate the change they wish to lead.

As a jaguar personality on the hunt, you can disrupt your ecosystem. Before you launch out on the next hunt, remember to think about your impact. You may feel like the chameleons, sloths, and hippos are holding you back. But recall the old adage: If you think you are leading and no one is following, you are simply taking a walk.

> **Jaguars need to pace themselves when pursuing the change they desperately want.**

Remember, the jaguar is at the top of the food chain. You are an apex predator. This is great if you are a big cat in the wild. But being a jaguar type in the office can morph into an overconfidence that restricts your desire to listen and learn from others. Don't forget that each time you implement a change, it ripples throughout your ecosystem (your family, workplace, church, and community).

This is certain: jaguars will lead others. You have what it takes to help many around you find victory during times of change. But you need to pace yourself and be mindful of others. One thing that can help is reading books on team building and listening to people who value uplifting and equipping others. Make sure to have someone in your life who has the courage to tell you to slow down.

The Chameleon

LIVING IN FLORIDA, I have learned to love lizards. You might even say they've become part of my family. My cat loves to eat them. My dog loves to play with them. My boys love to torture their mom and sister with them. For my part, I'm convinced that every variety of lizard calls our place "home."

About 5,000 species of lizards exist in the world. They range from about an inch to the six-foot-long Komodo dragon. One of the coolest species is the chameleon. You've heard of these guys.

They have two abilities that will blow your mind. Chameleons have stereoscopic vision. Because of the shape of their eyes and the fact that each eye works independently, they can see 360 degrees around them at all times, which means they can see behind and in front simultaneously! They can observe all—literally all—the change going on around them in real time. If danger approaches, they can quickly spot it and head for safety. If a jaguar is chasing an antelope, a chameleon's left eye will see the running prey while his right eye will see the jaguar quickly closing the gap.

You already know their other cool ability: they can change color. This cloaking device obviously enhances their safety. It keeps them alive, but it correspondingly helps them thrive, as their color change also signals their availability at mating time. Mating, after all, is what keeps any species alive. Chameleons' adaptive ability is quick and intentional. As their environment changes, their camouflage does too. Change is how they survive and even flourish.

On Your Team

Think about yourself and the people around you. Does anyone resemble the chameleon? They seem unflappable through change. They may be facing challenges at home, at work, or at the doctor's office, yet they absorb it and even use it to their advantage. It's almost like they saw it all coming with their stereoscopic vision. Picture it: the technology department rolls out a new computer system. Most people walk away whining, but the chameleons leave the meeting smiling. They get to work. Before you know it, they have absorbed the new information, shifted their routine, and have mastered the system change.

Winning through change is part of chameleons' hardwiring. They rarely initiate change, but they sense when it is coming. They are good at adapting to it with a positive attitude, determination, confidence, and persistence.

The great things about chameleons:

- Inherent positive attitude toward change
- Quick response to change
- Effective team members
- Task-oriented during the process
- Deep-seated desire to "fit in"
- Some institutional memory

The not-so-great things about chameleons:

- Quietly blend in instead of leading during change
- Withhold input or suggestions
- Fade to the background in conflict
- Can get paralyzed while moving ahead without clear direction

A self-assessment is on the next page. Answer the questions honestly to discover your chameleon tendencies.

Self-Assessment

1. When faced with change, what statement best describes your feelings?

    4 Assessment mode kicks in.
    3 Let's get it done.
    2 I will survive.
    1 Not again.

2. When going through change, what is most true of you?

    4 I like to be in the front, but I do not have to be in charge.
    3 I like to lead.
    2 I want clear guidance and a timeline.
    1 I want to get through it so it goes away.

3. Think about the last major change you experienced. Looking back on it, what statement best describes how you walked through it?

    4 I wish I would've had more information from the beginning.
    3 I hurt some people along the way.
    2 I was able to complete it.
    1 I wish it had not happened.

4. How often do you initiate change when it is not necessary?

> 4 I execute many changes once I think them over.
> 3 If something is on my mind for a long time, I will make a change.
> 2 Hardly ever.
> 1 I cannot remember ever doing that.

5. Do you get bored if things remain the same?

> 4 Sometimes.
> 3 Often.
> 2 Not very often.
> 1 Almost never.

6. How would you prefer to move through your day?

> 4 Not seen and not heard.
> 3 Sometimes seen and heard.
> 2 When I have something to say, I need to be seen and heard.
> 1 I better be listened to.

Decoding Your Answers

Look back over your responses and add up your numbers. The closer you are to 24 means the closer you are to having the chameleon personality. If your core reaction to change is expressed with words like *calm, confident, reassured, adaptable*, and so on, you may be a chameleon. If you rarely feel tension related to change, you sound like this special lizard. And if you seem to see the good in change and find adaptation easy, then it's almost certain.

Life as a Chameleon

Chameleons like you tend to maintain good attitudes when challenged by change. They are hardwired to get better, not bitter. They have the special ability to see the entire playing field clearly. Seeing the past, present, and a glimpse of the future provides them with both confidence and comfort.

Chameleons are beautiful animals—and personality types. Celebrate who you are! But be careful in your changing environment. As you quickly adapt your values, principles, and personality, do not change the essence of who you are. Your tendency may be to change simply to fit the change. Pump your chameleon brakes! Evaluate the requirements of the change in front of you.

Once you've been through a change, be on your guard. If you are not aware, your ability to quickly adapt may cause you to leave behind important lessons and values. As you move ahead, take what you have learned with you. Your tendency may be to forget what you have learned, both good and bad, and jump head-first into what is facing you.

One more thing: be aware that not everyone in your ecosystem is as adaptable as you. Be patient with them. Help them with perspective. After all, you have stereoscopic vision; you may see things that others do not. Have the courage to make your observations known. Others' reluctance may be an eyesight problem: they are unable to see the past and the future like you can. Use your positive attitude to drive the momentum of change in constructive directions.

> **One more thing: be aware that not everyone in your ecosystem is as adaptable as you. Be patient with them. Help them with perspective.**

By now, you may have concluded you are neither a jaguar nor a chameleon. It is possible you are a sloth. (Before you pout at my sloth suggestion, at least read the section about this maligned species!)

The Sloth

THINK ABOUT THIS: no other animal has ever had their name converted into one of the seven deadly sins! Everyone knows what we mean when we call someone slothful: slow, sluggish, and sleepy. A sloth will live from ten to thirty years—a long life for an animal—but no wonder: he sleeps up to eighteen hours a day. (That's more than my teenage daughter sleeps!) Healthy sloths will consume more than a minute climbing six feet. And not only do they move slowly externally, they also move slowly internally: it takes sloths up to a month to digest their food.

You get the idea. Sloths sleep their lives away and move at a glacial pace. But here's something you may not know: a sloth will spend most of its life clinging to a tree branch. The *same* branch. With toes that are long, hooked, and clawlike, sloths have the ability to lock around a tree limb and hang in the same spot for weeks on end. Offer them a nicer branch, and they may not even acknowledge the suggestion to change. Their ability to stay locked in place is hardwired into their DNA. Sloths have even been known to die and still be hanging on the same branch (kind of brings new meaning to the old military phrase "Die in place"[xi]). A sloth will move for three reasons only: danger, food, and mating.

On Your Team

You might be thinking about people you know who fit the sloth category—not in the traditional insulting way, of course. They may be slow movers, but they are harmless and lovable, and their unimposing demeanor makes you like (and sometimes pity) them. Truth be told, you might even consider yourself a sloth.

In the jungle of change, the sloth will cling motionless to the status quo until a strong enough motivation for change stares them in the face. In the wild, this motivation is most likely an exhausted food source, but on your team, the sloth may embrace change only when faced with "change or get fired."

The great things about sloths:

- Steady performers
- Rarely challenge authority or the status quo
- Kind and upbeat, even if slow
- Can appear confident
- Will not drag others down

- Great institutional memory
- Will ask great questions
- Will help define a clear plan

The not-so-great things about sloths:

- Can appear disconnected from the need for change
- Can be gripped with insecurity, fear, and attitude issues
- May suffer from "the sky is falling" syndrome

It's important for you to know if you are hardwired as a sloth. A self-assessment is on the next page. Answer the questions honestly to discover your sloth tendencies.

Self-Assessment

1. Do you like to keep the same pace of life during change?

> 4 Always.
> 3 Mostly.
> 2 Not really. I can see the need to speed up.
> 1 Never! I want to get it done.

2. Does the prospect of a big change upset you?

> 4 Yep, almost always.
> 3 Always. For sure.
> 2 Not really if I see the need.
> 1 Never, I'm always up for a challenge.

3. When going through change, how aware are you of others and their feelings and struggles?

> 4 That concerns me a lot.
> 3 I think about it some if the change will impact people I know.
> 2 I think about what I can do to lessen the blow on people.
> 1 I do not think about it much.

4. Do you find sameness comfortable?

> 4 Absolutely.
> 3 Most of the time.
> 2 Sometimes.
> 1 Nope.

5. Looking back on the last change you went through, how would you grade yourself?

> 4 I moved slowly and deliberately.
> 3 I resisted until I saw the reason for it.
> 2 I moved pretty well, learning and growing as I needed to.
> 1 I owned it.

6. During a change, do you often reflect on the past, what things were like before the change?

> 4 Often.
> 3 Sometimes, if I need more explanation for the change.
> 2 Rarely.
> 1 Never.

Decoding Your Answers

Total your numbers. The closer you are to 24, the more sloth-like tendencies you have. If you'd prefer to cling to your routines and continue moving forward with the plans and pace you have set for yourself, you're probably a sloth.

Life as a Sloth

Never mind what people say about sloths. You are slow and methodical, yes, but your pace may reduce the risk of mistakes. However, you must acknowledge that the world is rapidly changing and that many of those changes are necessary. In fact, adjusting to change too slowly has been the nail in the coffin for many companies. Additionally, workers who fail to change are often the victims of layoffs.

Even though it's difficult, move through the necessary changes, leveraging the way you are hardwired to your advantage. As you move slowly through the changes, share your insights with others. Help the jaguars see that their rapid pace may have precluded some necessary considerations. Help the chameleons see that changing simply to fit in can come at the cost of abandoning important values.

> *Never mind what people say about sloths. You are slow and methodical, yes, but your pace may reduce the risk of mistakes.*

But look in the mirror, too. You may instinctively resist change out of insecurity, fear, or the attitude that "We've always done it this way." In and of itself, the old way may not suffice in an ever-changing world.

Know that the call to change will stir anxiety and perhaps even feelings of depression. So when you're undergoing change, learn a lesson from your jungle counterparts: get plenty of sleep and maintain a diet that gives you consistent energy throughout the day.

Read books about personal development and leadership. Interact with the other species in your ecosystem. You can learn from them, and they can learn from you. Ask them questions and examine how they navigate change. Start expanding your appreciation of it, and as you become more responsive to change, you may even learn to embrace it.

Jaguars, chameleons, and sloths. The jungle is getting full. Let's add another animal to the ecosystem: the hippo.

The Hippopotamus

THERE ARE FEW ANIMALS more recognizable than the ancient hippo. *Hippopotamus* is a Greek word meaning "horse of the river," and that's an apt description. Now let's be clear: hippos do not actually live in the jungle in their natural state, but they *do* live in our jungle. You may be one or you may lead one, so let's discuss the hippo. Male hippos tip the scale at 9,900 pounds, and females can weigh up to 3,000 pounds. As animals living in the wild, they live a long time—up to forty-five years. They live in communities of twenty to thirty hippos, called *bloats*. These bloats usually have one male who calls the shots as they protect a specific stretch of a river. Hippos are territorially aggressive, and their species has not changed much over the years. In fact, they seem impervious to change.

Hippos seem concerned about two things: laying around and eating. They lay still in the water and mud during the day to protect their sensitive skin from the sun and to conserve energy. The lack of movement helps balance their need for food. After all, a hippo needs to consume at least one percent of his body weight a day to maintain his enormous waistline.

As the sun goes down, a hippo will graze, eating 30 to 120 pounds of grass, plants, and fruit. You might say hippos move only when their total and complete existence depends on it. Hippos are hardwired to avoid changing their stretch of the river because moving expends precious calories. You get the picture. No one is going to convince these beasts to change their ecosystem unless their food supply dwindles.

On Your Team

Now I'm sure you know that if you call a coworker a hippo, you will probably get slapped. But you undoubtedly know someone who is hippo-like when it comes to change. Maybe it's you! And it's perfectly okay if it is.

Hippos resist change. The world comes, and the world goes—and hippos remain the same. They guard their boundaries with aggressive words and grumpy actions. Sometimes they opt for a passive-aggressive approach, not only holding their ground against change but also gathering a herd in resistance. Hippos have big mouths with dangerous teeth,

> *Hippos resist change. The world comes, and the world goes—and hippos remain the same.*

and they use their voices to argue for the status quo. Even if their food supply is depleted and change is inevitable for survival, they will complain every step of the way.

The great things about hippos:

- Great institutional memory
- Influencers of others
- Eager to share their thoughts
- Dependable and strong
- Intentional when asked to change
- Demand good reasoning for change

The not-so-great things about hippos:

- Resistant to a reasonable call to change
- Eager to convince others to oppose change
- Influential because of their long history
- Will often complain
- They may say, "We have never done it that way before"

It's important for you to know if you are hardwired as a hippo. A self-assessment is on the next page. Answer the questions honestly to discover your hippo-like tendencies.

Self-Assessment

1. Do you consider change a waste of time and avoid it?

> 4 Always. I choose change only when I need it to survive.
> 3 Most of the time.
> 2 I do not love it, but I can deal with it.
> 1 I run toward change.

2. What feelings do you have when going through changes?

> 4 Resentment, frustration, and anger.
> 3 Annoyance, confusion, and exhaustion.
> 2 Curiosity, concern, and steadiness.
> 1 Eagerness, excitement, and readiness.

3. Do you find yourself resisting innovative ideas because you don't want to spend the time and effort that change requires?

> 4 Always (unless my job is on the line).
> 3 Yes, until I see the advantage of the change.
> 2 No, I embrace change and do what I can to make it work for me.
> 1 No. I'm always ready for new ideas and the change they can bring.

4. Have you ever initiated an optional, unnecessary change?

> 4 Never, I hate the thought.
> 3 Maybe.
> 2 Yes, but with a strategic end in mind.
> 1 Often.

5. During corporate change, do you guard your area of responsibility with an unyielding tenacity?

> 4 To the death.
> 3 Yes, but I will let go eventually.
> 2 Sort of, only until I get everything in order.
> 1 Nope.

6. Have you ever thought or said, "But we have never done it like that before"?

> 4 Yep, often.
> 3 Sometimes, but not so much.
> 2 Maybe, but not often.
> 1 Maybe by accident.

Decoding Your Answers

Now add your numbers. The closer to 24 you are, the more hippo-like tendencies you have. If you find yourself avoiding change or being negative toward those who desire change, you are probably a hippo. If have often said or thought the words "We have never done it like that before," then you have hippo-like tendencies.

Life as a Hippo

It may sound harsh to think of yourself as someone who has dropped anchor and won't move. But institutional anchors have this positive element: they prevent mission and institutional amnesia. At the same time, be careful not to justify a negative attitude toward change in the name of defending a boundary.

The world is changing, and hippos, with their natural opposition to change, have earned a spot on a notorious list: vulnerable to extinction. What's true for hippos in the wild is true for their human equivalents. Resistance to a rapidly changing workplace (and an aggressive reaction to the prospect) threatens their survival.

The solution begins with awareness. Read about the changes coming in your industry. Develop friendships with people who love change. You may pick up valuable insights from someone with a different change type. Finally, begin to identify *why* you're so averse to change. List some of the changes from your past that worked out well. You may find changes in the past were not as bad as you imagined.

> **But institutional anchors have this positive element: they prevent mission and institutional amnesia.**

After all, your survival depends on your ability to change.

There's one more thing hippos need to be aware of: their big teeth. When hippos in the wild feel threatened, they often become aggressive. And because they are equipped with teeth that are more than a foot long, they can rip into others. It's not pretty. If you know your reaction to change is hippo-ish, keep watch on your temper. Be aware of how you treat others when faced with changes beyond your control.

Conclusion

JAGUARS, CHAMELEONS, sloths, and hippos. The jungle is full of these four species who collectively face change. But independently, each will approach it differently. Jaguars will run after the prey. Chameleons will crave adaptation. Sloths will hang on for dear life. Hippos will rarely move.

While it may seem unlikely for these animals to befriend one another in a jungle, they have discovered how to live in harmony. After all, jaguars don't feast on sloths, and chameleons stay out of reach of the hippo's teeth.

Just like our jungle counterparts, we benefit from sharing our ecosystems with different personality types. It may sound like we need to learn from these animals, (and we do), but it is worth noting that they could learn from us. Humans possess a host of abilities that animals don't. We can read, study, analyze, interact, and change. It is possible for humans to learn from one another, to value one another's similarities and differences, and to imitate the strengths of those who are different from us. The lower species cannot do that.

My strategy in this volume was simple: help you have fun thinking about yourself and those around you. But as simplistic as the quizzes and explanations may have been, remember that we are complex people. Just because you exhibit a certain change type doesn't mean that you cannot grow and learn to adapt to change differently. As you may have noticed, my end-of-chapter advice for each change type urged you to expose yourself to the other species—to learn from their strengths and see how imitation may help you eliminate some of your weaknesses.

The ultimate goal of this book has been to help you understand the jungle of change so you are better able to adapt to it and lead others through it. I believe being a better version of yourself makes the jungle better for all its inhabitants.

Nature or Nurture

All of us would agree that some people move and adapt to change better and more quickly than others. Some of that is due to our hardwiring—our nature. But part of it also comes from our environment—our nurture. Given enough time, nature and nurture combine to become our internal foundation that is impacted by and reacts to change. Granted, there may not be much you can do to influence your nature part. Maybe, for as long as you can remember, you have loved the thought of something new and different. Or maybe, for every new idea that has come along, you have always resisted and asked why it was necessary. We all have our hardwiring. It is neither good nor bad; it simply is.

Fortunately, the nurture part allows us to grow and develop. Perhaps we've learned to resist change because of a negative incident in our formative years. Maybe we grew up with a jaguar. Every new and exciting idea that came along was pounced on. Maybe that led to some instability and uncertainty in your home. Or maybe you grew up in a home with a hippo. You sat helplessly and watched great opportunities pass you by. How we were nurtured in the past can't be changed, but we can determine to address our ruts, rituals, relationships, and realities to alter the habits we settled into because of our past.

If you desire to grow through change, to get better with processing and leading through change, you need a few habits. First, know how you are hardwired. This little book should have helped some with that part. Second, position yourself around people who are not like you. Develop friendships with the different change types. Learn to value their strengths. Third, be a reader, and read broadly. The information you gather from other types of people will begin to transform you. Finally, put yourself in uncomfortable situations. If you're a jaguar, put yourself in a situation where patience and institutional memory is needed. If you're a hippo, seek situations that are fast-paced to grow in your ability to accept and adapt to change.

Change can be a challenge, but it is possible to adapt, even in our ever-changing world. Be honest enough to determine your primary personality type: jaguar, chameleon, sloth, or hippo. Celebrate your strengths and identify your weaknesses. Then have the courage to learn from others around you and let them learn from you.

Change is inevitable. Growth is optional.

Choose growth.

Acknowledgements

I want to thank my good friend Dan Doster who pushed me to finish this project and my longtime friend Dr. Chris Stephens for years of friendship.

I also want to thank Eddie Wiggins for providing the opportunity to present this information all over the country.

Finally, to the elders and congregation of Grace Fellowship: without you guys, I wouldn't even be in the game. Thank you!

Visit ChangeIsAJungle.com

to find out more about Terry Wright, to book him as a keynote speaker, or to request that he leads a "Change Is a Jungle" conference for your organization.

Thank you!

Endnotes

[i] Instead of attending college, physicians attended medical schools, many of which were condemned in the press and by the government as substandard.

[ii] *Dictionary.com*, s.v. "change."

[iii] John F. Kennedy, "Address in the Assembly Hall at the Paulskirche in Frankfurt (266)," June 25, 1963, *Public Papers of the Presidents: John F. Kennedy, 1963.*

[iv] *The Wonder Years.*

[v] "The Model T," Ford, accessed July 11, 2023, https://corporate.ford.com/articles/history/the-model-t.html.

[vi] Jeff Rubingh, "A Rollout Like No Other," Technology Created, December 5, 2012, https://technologycreated.com/2012/12/02/a-rollout-like-no-other/.

[vii] *The Merriam-Webster's Dictionary*, s.v. "jungle."

[viii] Robert H. Schuller, "It Takes Guts to Get Out of the Ruts," Brainyquote, accessed July 11, 2023, https://www.brainyquote.com/quotes/robert_h_schuller_380575.

[ix] *The Merriam-Webster's Dictionary*, s.v. "jungle."

[x] Rick Warren, interview by Kim Lawton, *Religion & Ethics Newsweekly*, PBS, September 1, 2006, https://www.pbs.org/wnet/religionandethics/2006/09/01/september-1-2006-rick-kay-warren-extended-interview/3647/.

[xi] "Die in place" (DIP) is military slang for the order to hold your ground even if attacked by a formidable force.

Made in the USA
Columbia, SC
10 April 2024